HYGGE CHRISTMAS

CUTE & COZY CHRISTMAS COLORING BOOK

THIS BOOK BELONGS TO

_____

Fuzzy Pals Coloring Book Series

Published in 2024 by
BRIGHTME Publishing Inc.

Imprint: Fuzzy Pals Coloring

Fuzzy Pals Coloring is an imprint of BRIGHTME Publishing Inc.

For information about permission to reproduce selections from this book, please contact Fuzzy Pals Coloring at contact@fuzzypalscoloring.com

First Edition: September 2024
Visit our website at www.FuzzyPalsColoring.com

TEST COLOR PAGE

THANK YOU FOR CHOOSING OUR COLORING BOOK!

YOUR REVIEW MEANS THE WORLD TO US!

If you enjoyed this book, we'd be so grateful if you could leave a review on Amazon. Your feedback is super important—it not only helps others find and love our books but also encourages us to keep creating more cute and fun designs just for you!

THANK YOU FOR SUPPORTING OUR SMALL BUSINESS!

JOIN US ON TIKTOK!

SCAN ME

TEST COLOR PAGE

GET 30 BONUS COLORING PAGES WORTH $59.99 FOR FREE!

SCAN ME

We're excited to offer you an exclusive set of 30 beautifully designed coloring pages, completely free! Originally valued at $59.99, these pages are yours to download by simply scanning the QR code.

HAPPY COLORING!

PROTECT YOUR PAGES FOR A BETTER COLORING EXPERIENCE

Due to the limited paper options available on Amazon, we have selected a standard quality paper to keep the book affordable. This paper is perfect for use with colored pencils. However, if you are using alcohol-based markers, please place a blank sheet of thicker paper behind the page you are coloring to prevent any bleed-through. We appreciate your understanding and hope you enjoy your coloring experience!

SIMPLY PLACE A SHEET OF PAPER

WE APPRECIATE YOUR UNDERSTANDING!

THANK YOU!

Made in United States
Orlando, FL
21 November 2024

54244620R00050